AF407092

SHADES & SHADOWS

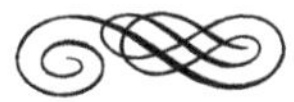

KATIE JACOBSON

For my dear, unwavering friends and loved ones.
This one is for you.

Thank you.

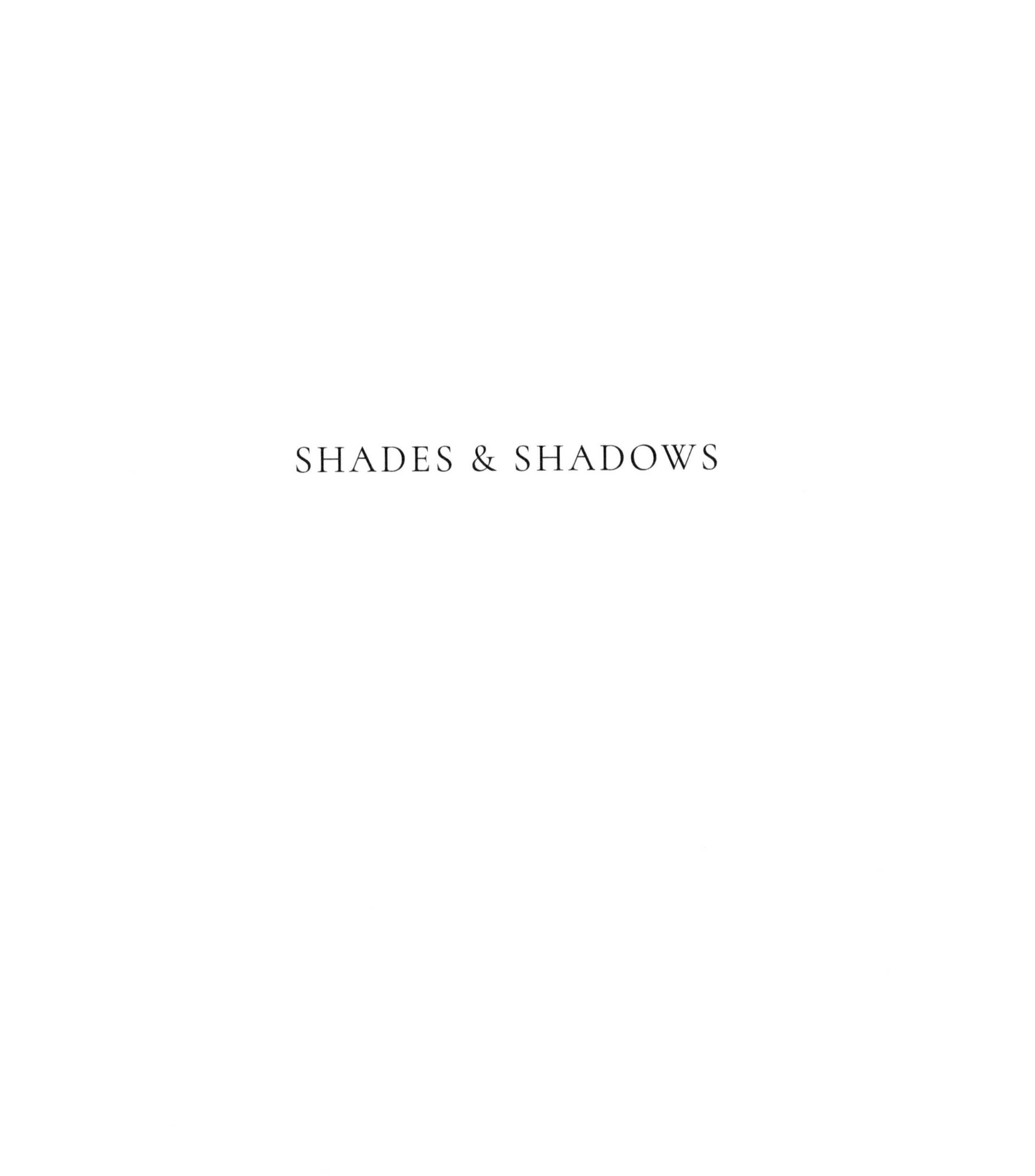

SHADES & SHADOWS

PART ONE

THE SHARPENER

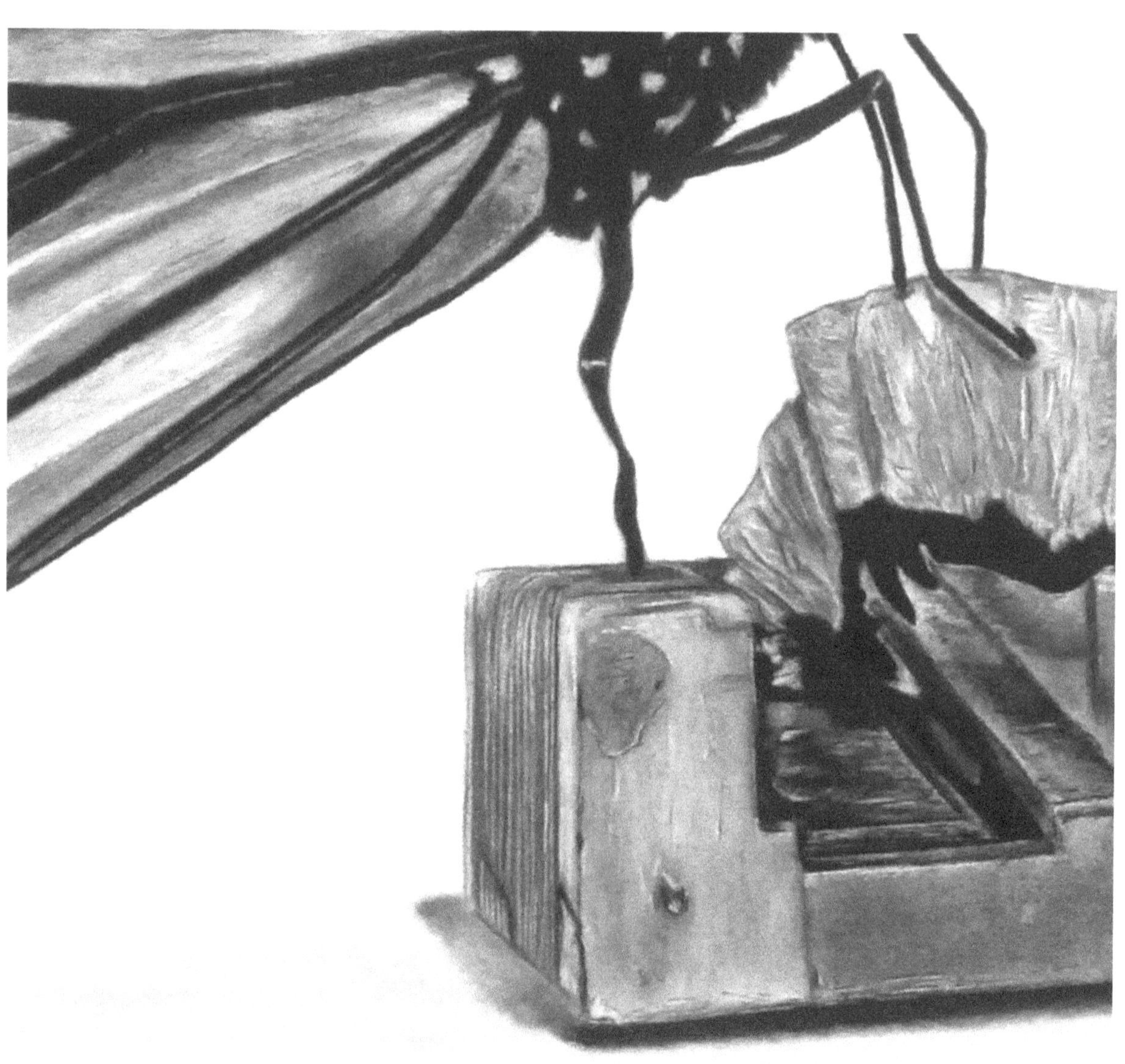

THE SHARPENER

Traveling through life, we hone our inner toolkit of skills, ensuring we're prepared for the inevitable moments that arise.

By attentively observing the dull aspects of life and proactively adapting to stay at our peak, we can cultivate a sharp, agile mindset that empowers us to excel in even the most challenging situations.

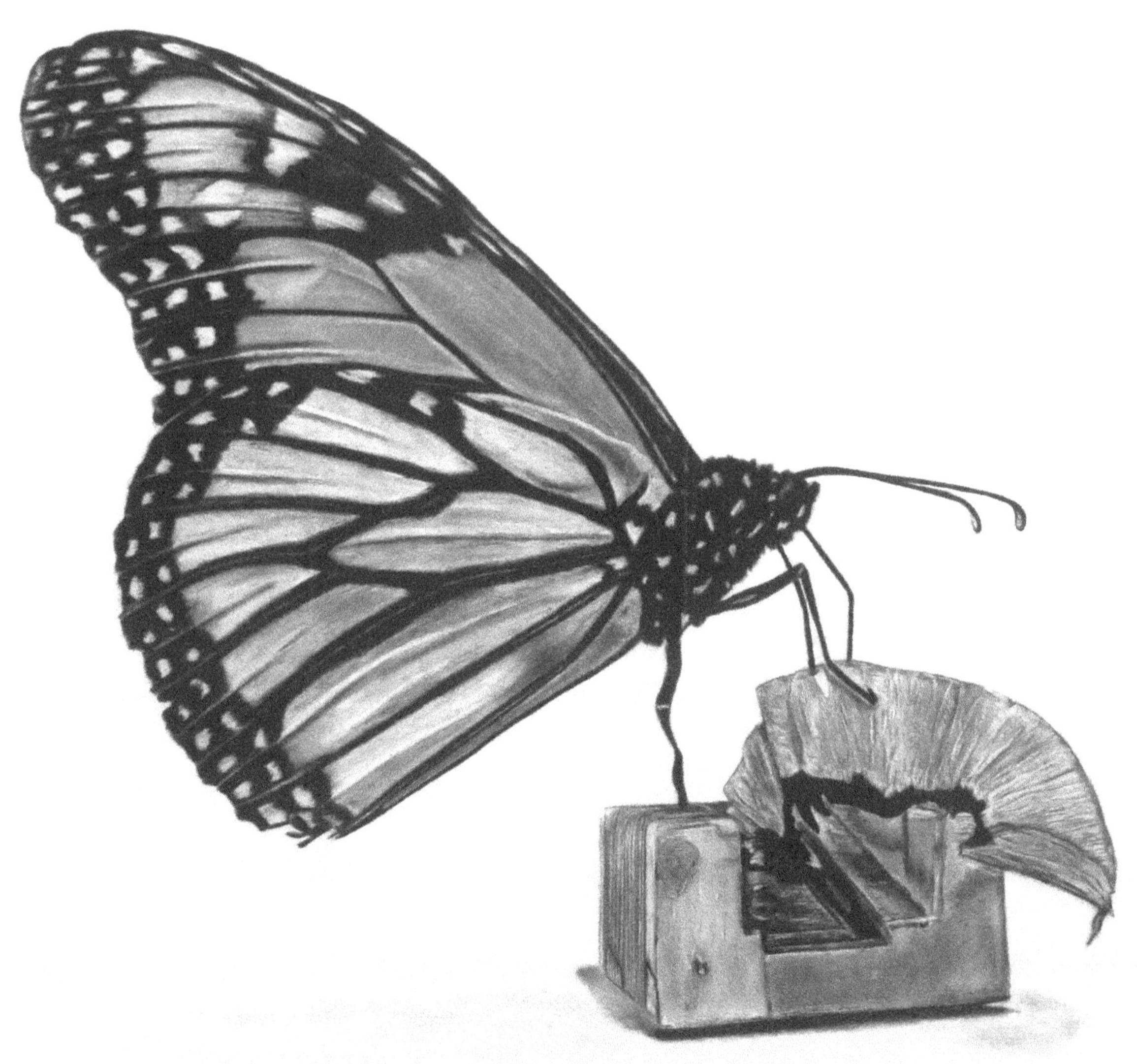

THE SHARPENER

THE IDEA COMES TO YOU

An idea might come, and you'll be met with having no idea how to act upon it. Recognize that there is no wrong place to start. Just start.

We may struggle with the desire to know everything from the outset. This can often lead to analysis paralysis and stagnation.

The true value lies in learning from the inevitable missteps we'll make along the way and incorporating those lessons into future decisions.

Repetition, reflection, and time are the ingredients needed to fully absorb the wisdom gained from our mistakes. This continuous process allows us to refine our approach and make meaningful progress.

PART TWO

THE PAINTBRUSH

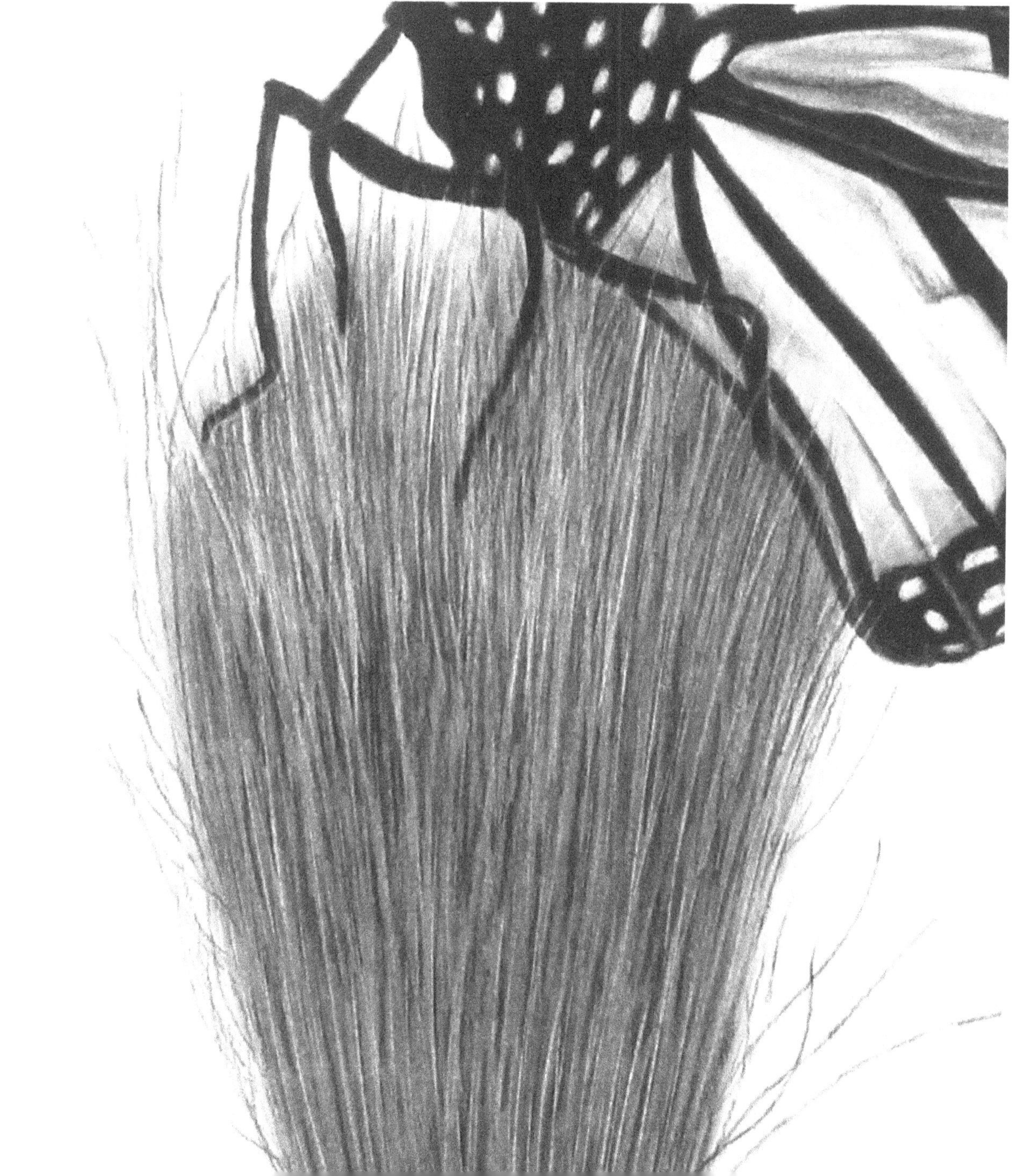

THE PAINTBRUSH

As we contemplate the fragile yet exquisite bristles of life, we're reminded of the beauty that

arises from delicacy and vulnerability.

In this realm of freedom, we find the courage to express ourselves authentically and

acknowledge that our potential is limitless, enabling

us to grow into whoever we choose to be.

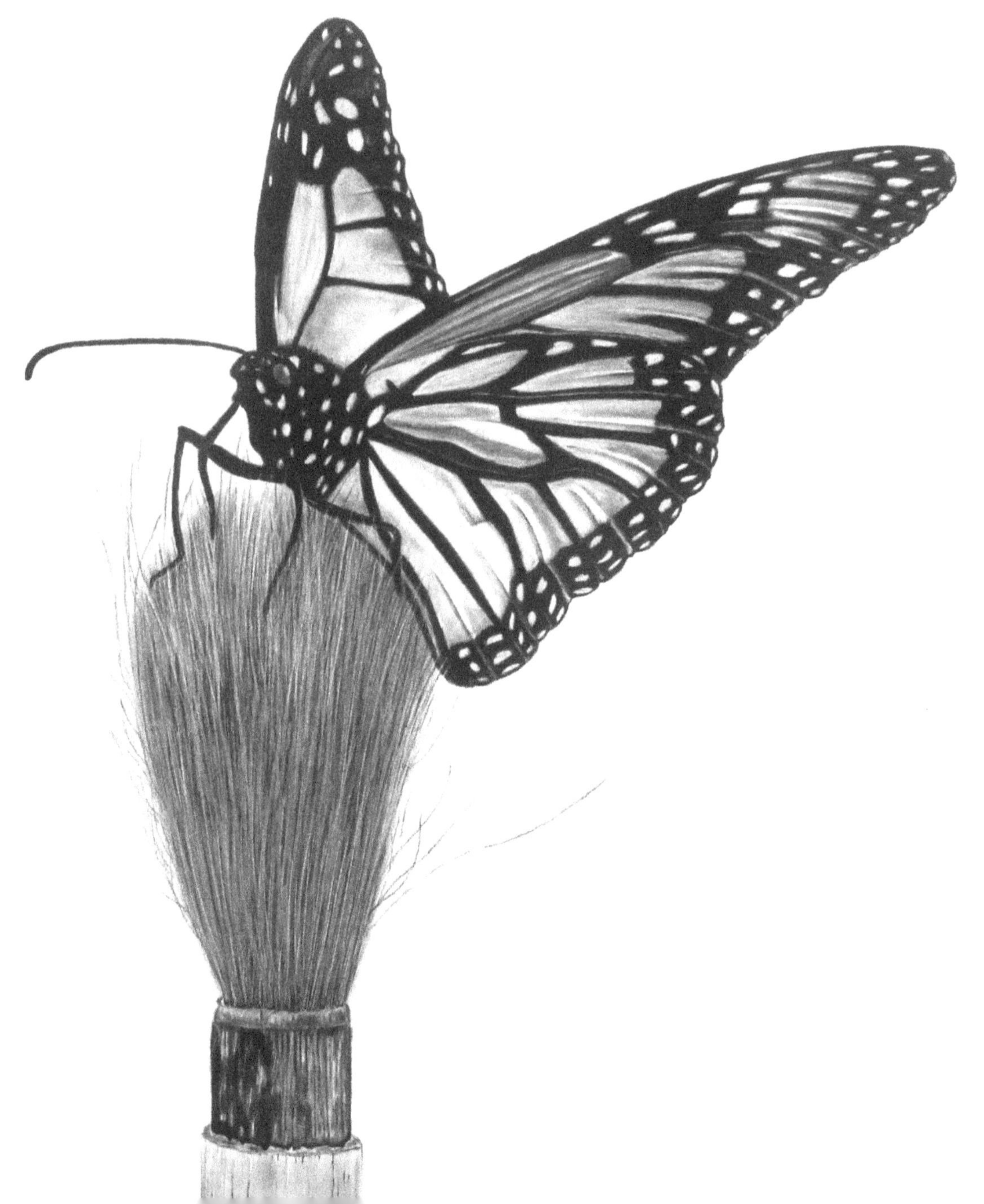

THE PAINTBRUSH

FEW WILL UNDERSTAND

Some may attempt to discourage you from embarking on unconventional paths.

They may perceive your decisions as odd or reckless, stemming from a place of genuine concern and a desire to protect you. However, be assured that you possess the resilience and adaptability to navigate uncharted territory.

By stepping outside the boundaries of the norm, you'll acquire valuable life skills that cannot be taught in a classroom, much less within the safety of the cocoon. Along the way, you'll encounter challenges that will test your mettle. By maintaining an unwavering belief in yourself and your abilities, you'll uncover opportunities and experiences that far surpass your wildest dreams.

Remember, it's often the boldest strokes that create the most breathtaking masterpieces.

Embrace the unknown, trust your instincts, and watch as your life unfolds in ways you never imagined.

PART THREE

THE CHARCOAL

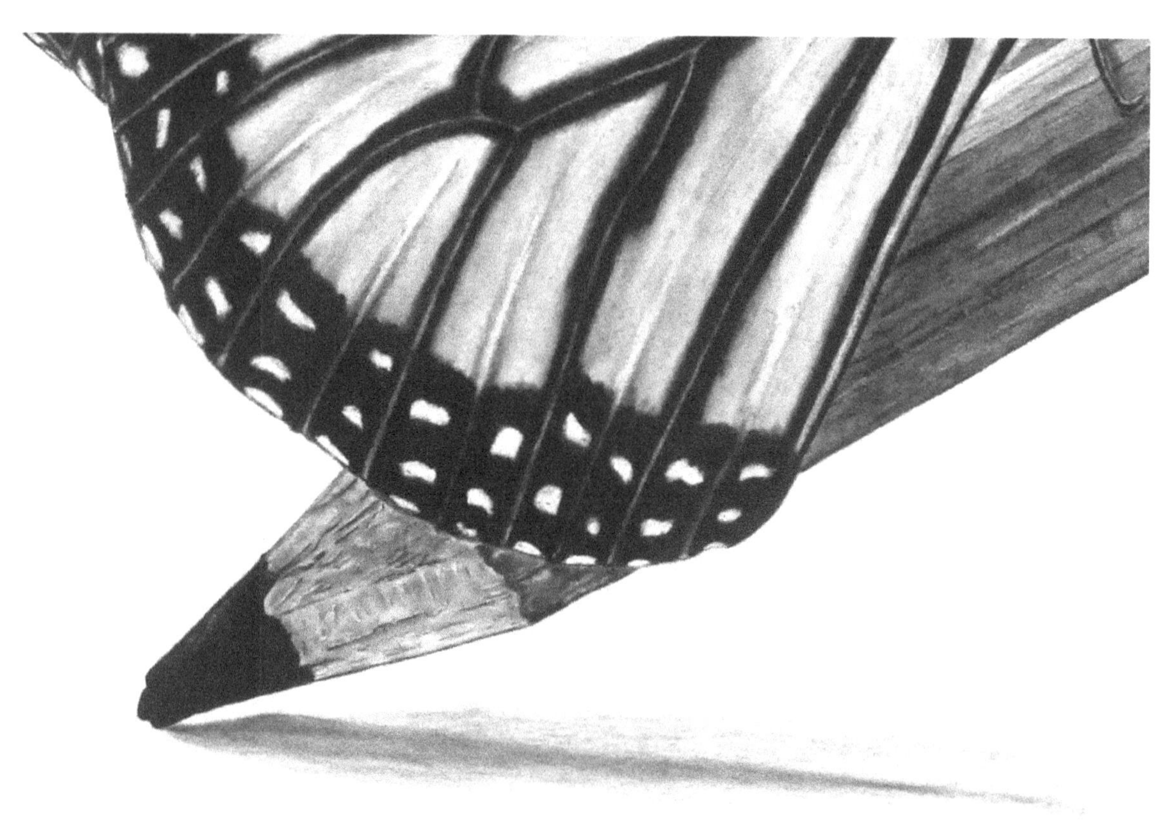

THE CHARCOAL

Despite the small things that may chip away at you over time, maintain a sense of poise,

sharpness, and readiness to act.

Don't be afraid to step outside the boundaries and create your own trajectory.

Embrace the notion that it's essential to forge your own path and blur

the lines that confine you.

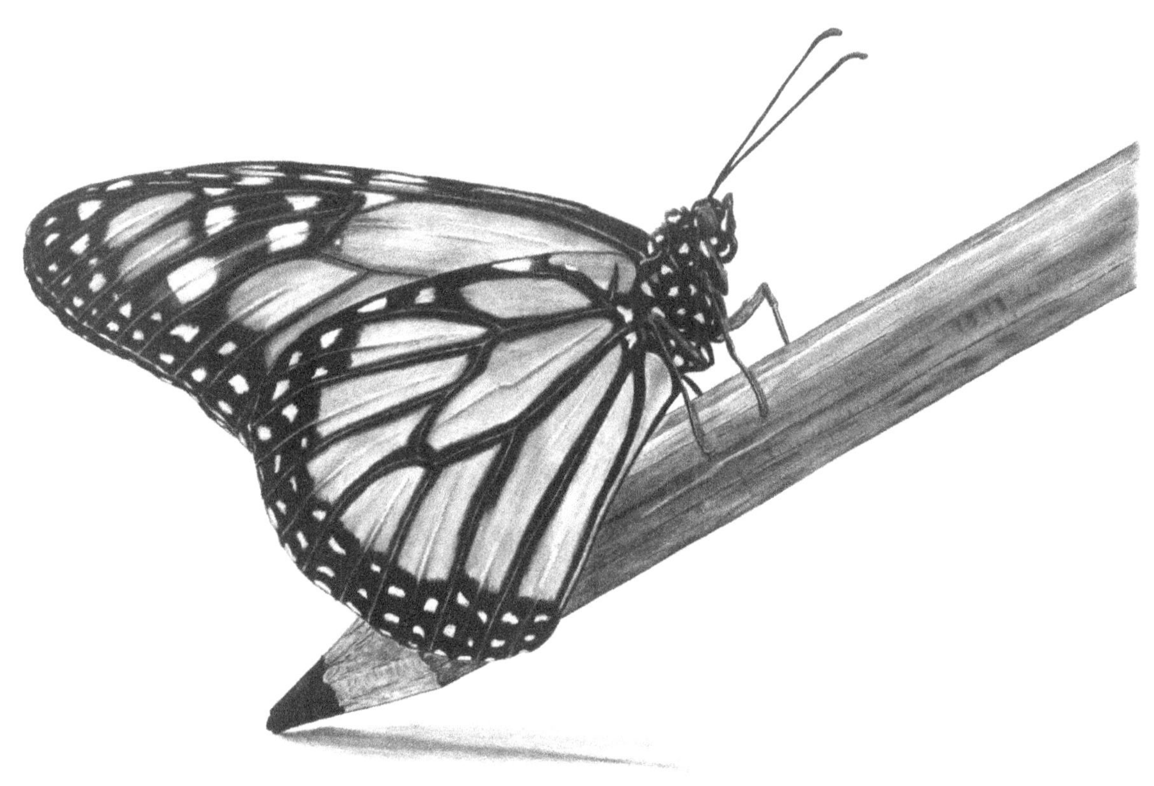

THE CHARCOAL

BELIEVE IN YOUR ABILITIES

Let this be a daily mantra: Remember the power within yourself to navigate life's twists and turns.

Reflect on how you've successfully navigated past challenges and triumphed over adversity. Be honest with yourself about the times you did not. Acknowledge the lessons taken from both. The self-awareness and confidence you'll gain from these lessons will empower you to face future obstacles with poise and resilience.

You don't need to be prepared for every scenario life throws your way. No matter how chaotic the situation may seem, remain level-headed and calm. This tranquility will have a soothing effect on those around you, preventing unnecessary tension and conflict.

A wise employer of mine often used this analogy: "You're like ducks. Calm on the surface, but paddling like hell underneath."

Be the duck: calm, composed, and resilient.

PART FOUR

THE PEG

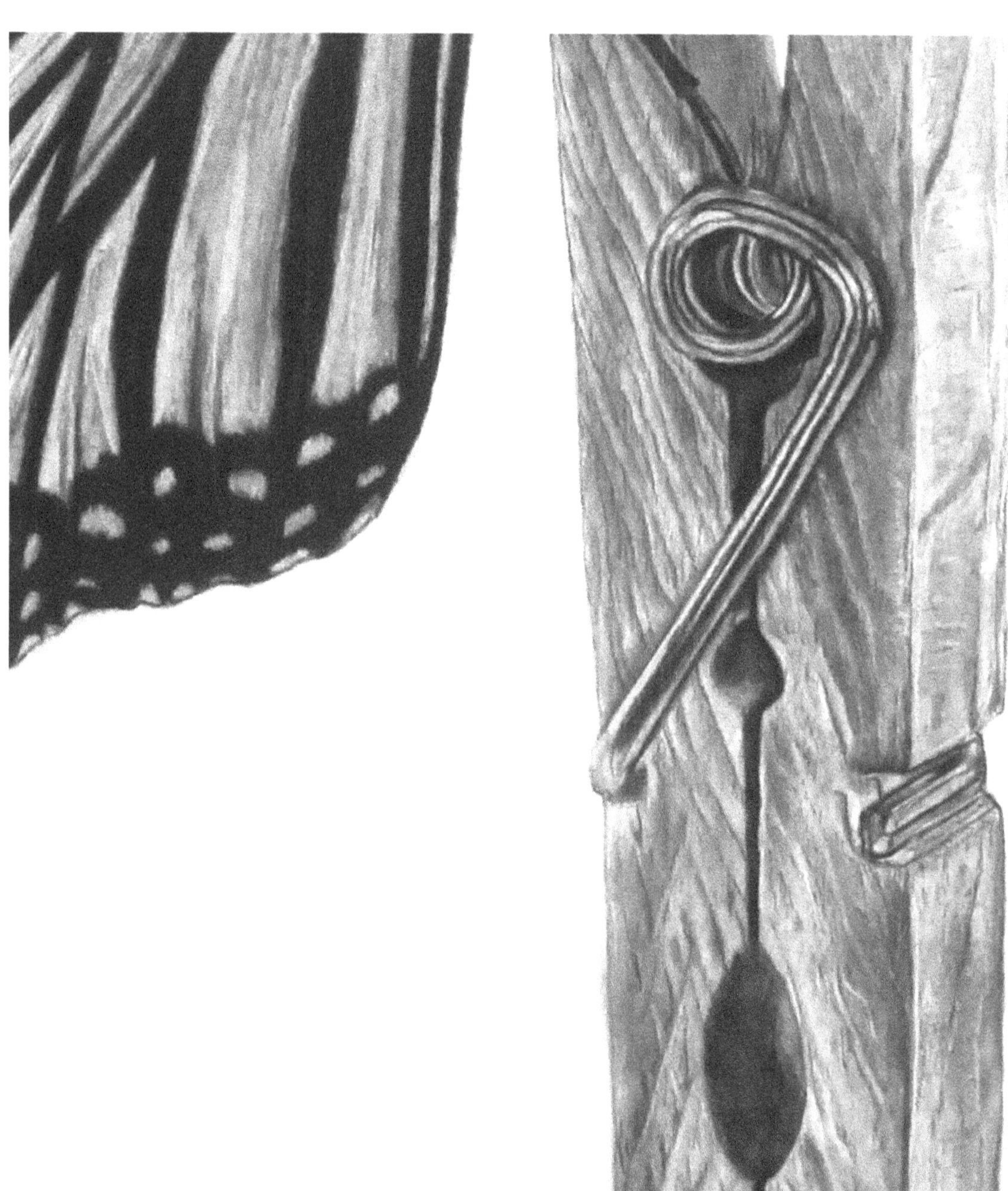

THE PEG

The humble wooden peg: standing tall and steadfast.

The peg is a reminder that you, too, possess the strength and resilience to weather life's

challenges with grace and determination.

Remember to not overcomplicate things and trust in your own ability to endure and thrive.

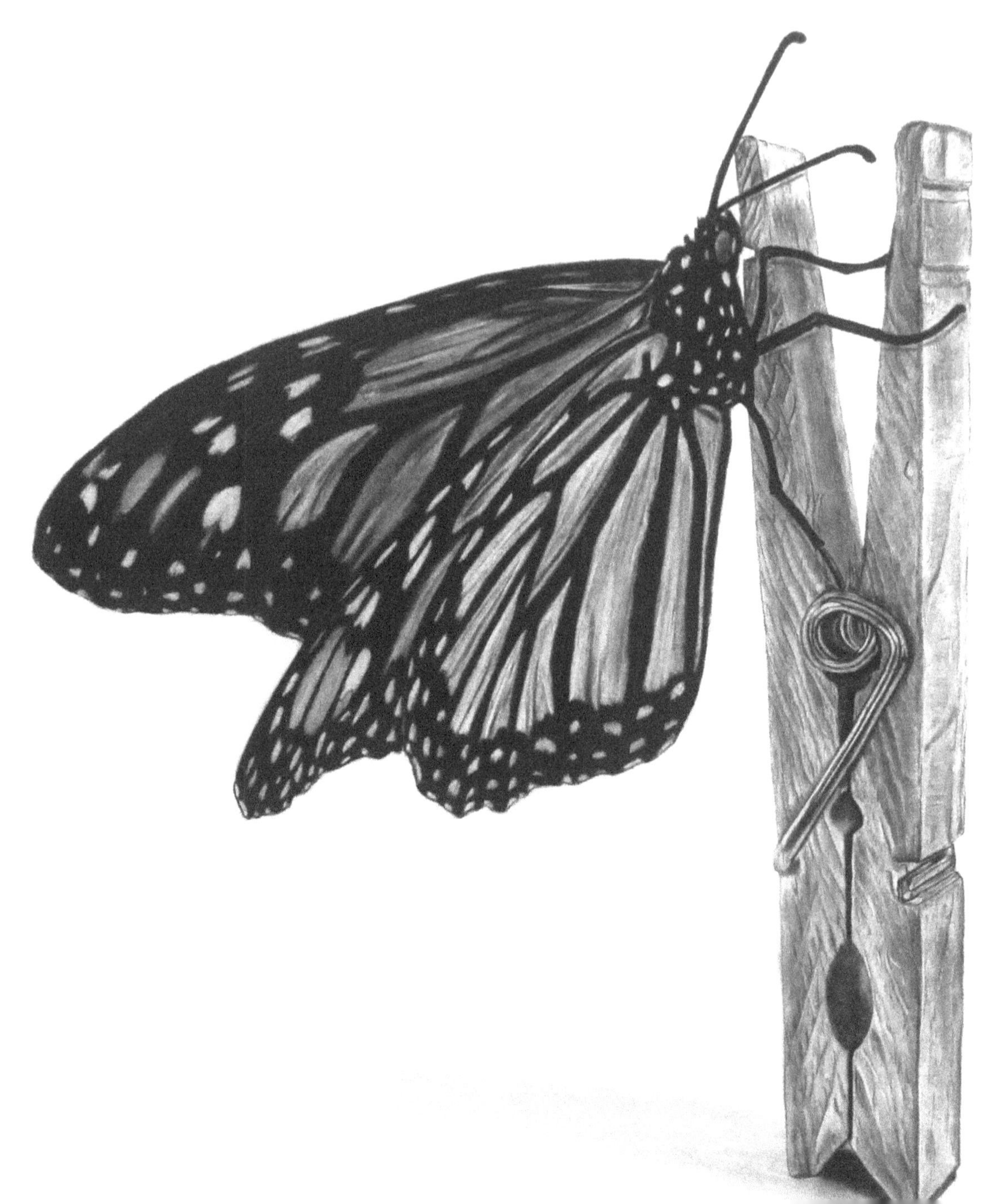

THE PEG

THERE WILL BE SACRIFICES

Be prepared for the sacrifices you will have to make along the way.

Living anywhere other than where you grew up will bring challenges. You'll miss out on cherished celebrations and events - birthdays, weddings, holidays, and more. This doesn't make you selfish. We mustn't allow others to convince us otherwise, as their expectations can be overwhelming. Break free from those constraints. Know that when you manage to attend these special occasions, they will be all the more precious.

Savor these moments, as they remind you of the importance of time and the value of presence. In the end, your sacrifices will be worth the experiences you gain and the relationships you nurture.

PART FIVE

THE ERASER

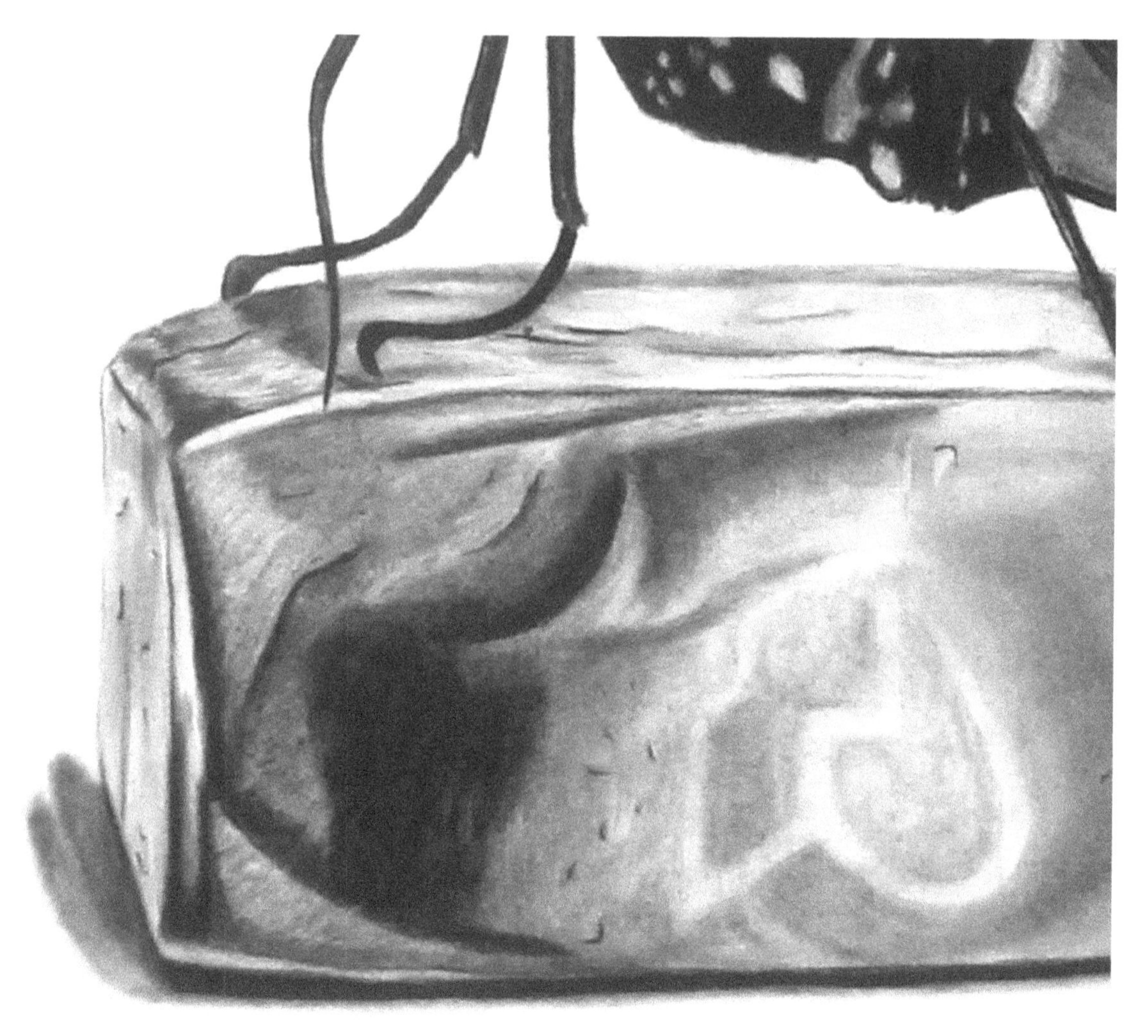

THE ERASER

We cannot erase our past; we can only embrace it, for it is the foundation upon which

you've built your life.

Lessons, both triumphant and challenging, have shaped you into the person you are today.

Harness these experiences to refine and enrich your life, becoming a better

version of yourself with each passing day.

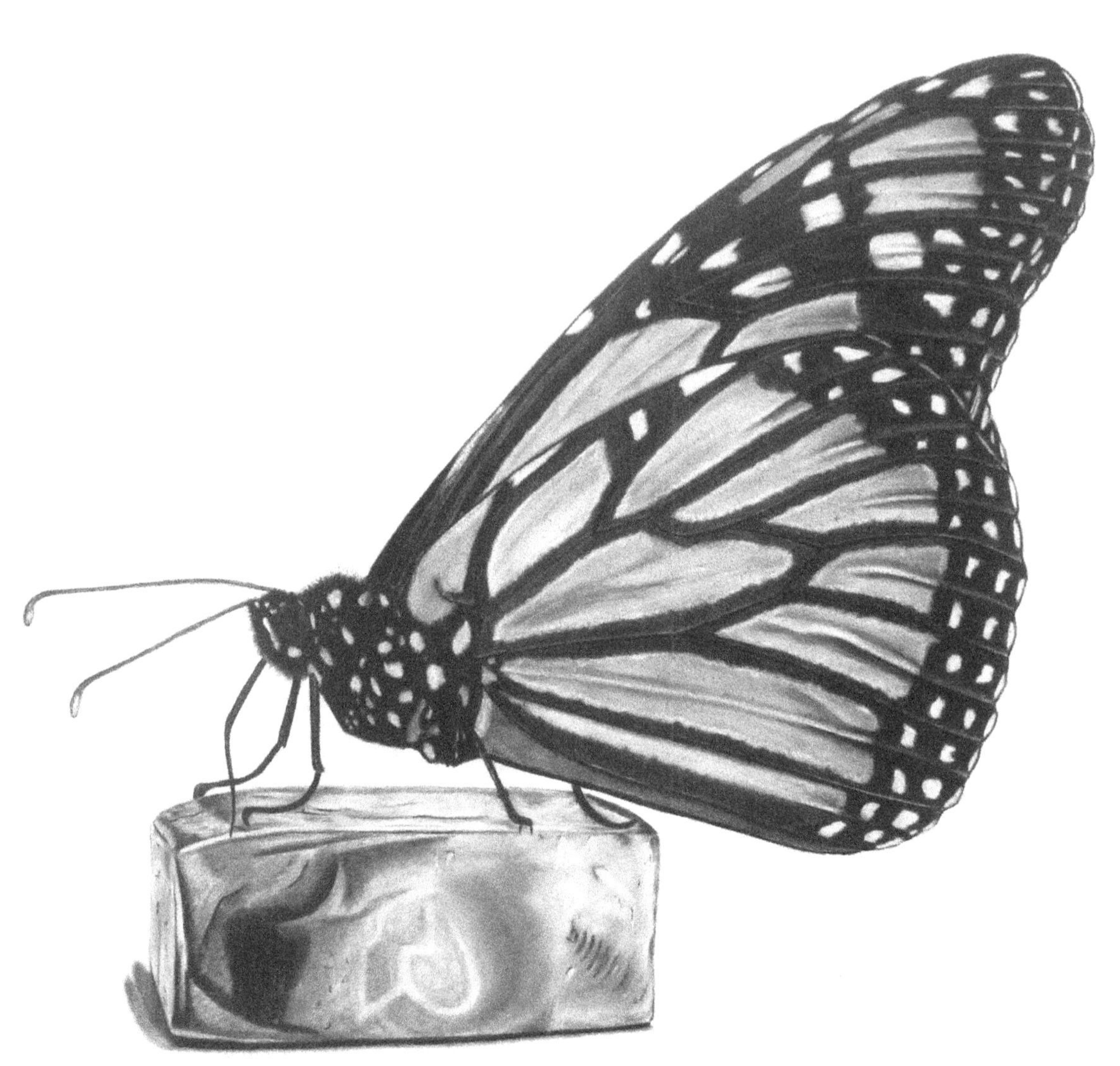

THE ERASER

THE IMPORTANCE OF PRIVACY

I've come to appreciate the importance of keeping my personal life private, particularly in the age and mirage of social media. I've found that disengaging from this aspect of modern life has brought me greater happiness and inner peace.

Embrace the authenticity that comes from disconnecting from the virtual world and focus on fostering genuine relationships that enrich your life. These good-faith connections, free from the influence of online opinions and comparisons, may become the most important in your life.

Some friends will become your chosen family. Treasure these relationships. Indeed, they are the ones who will be there for you, through thick and thin, without judgment. They'll also be the ones who are point-blank honest with you. They've witnessed you evolve throughout life, so they have an unparalleled understanding of you and what makes you tick.

Remember, you don't need to justify yourself to anyone, and the opinions of others should not define your self-worth. Maintain your integrity, and surround yourself with those who uplift and support you.

PART SIX

THE TAPE MEASURE

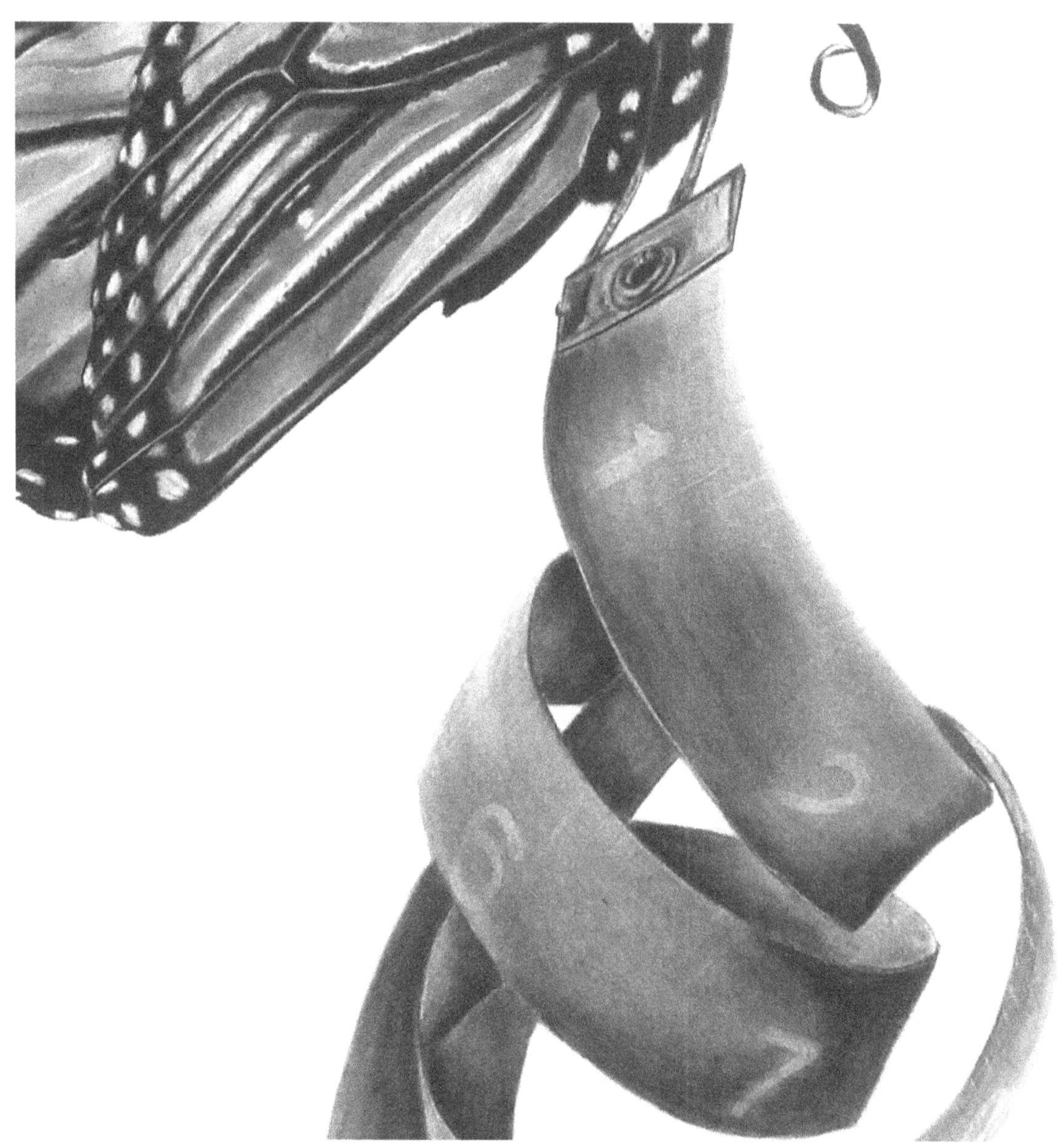

THE TAPE MEASURE

A reminder: don't measure yourself against others. We're all protagonists in our unique stories,

unfolding on our own timeline.

Embrace this truth, cultivate empathy, and remember that your path is yours alone.

Trust the process and find peace in each and every day.

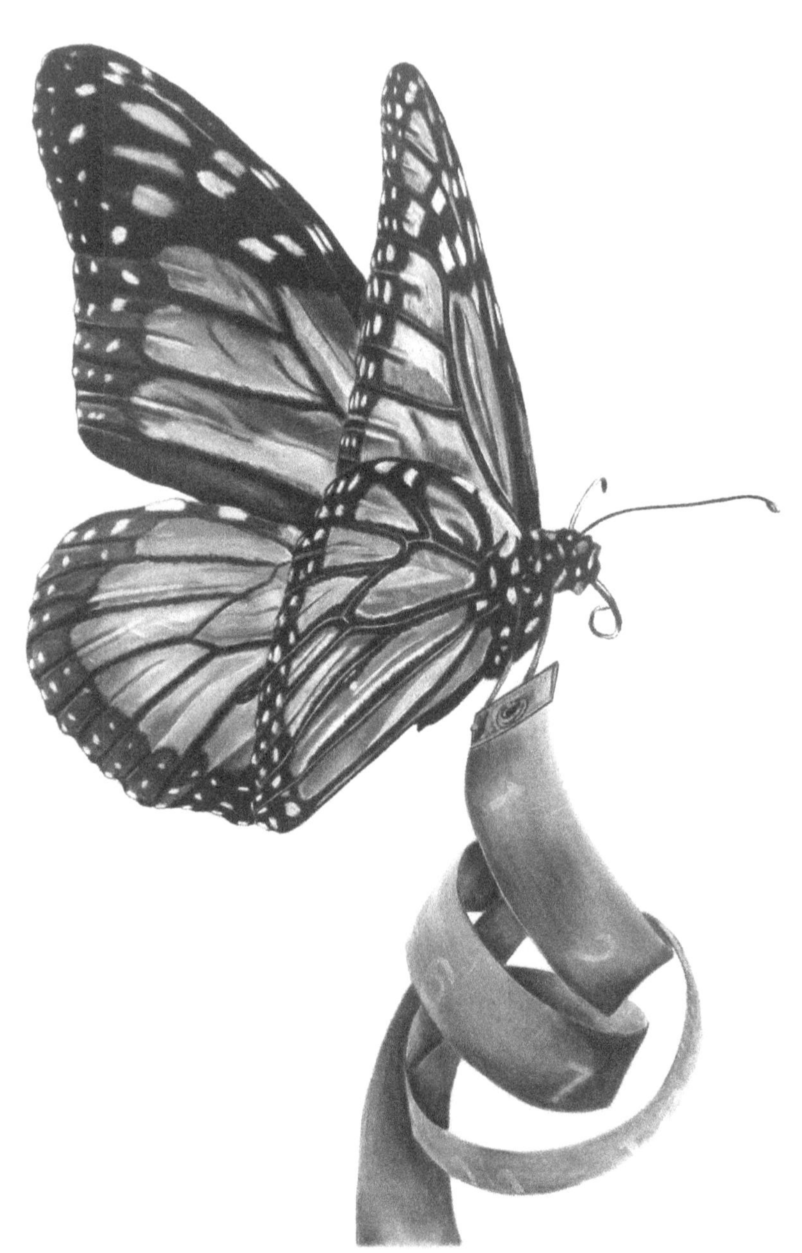

THE TAPE MEASURE

YOU'LL STRUGGLE TO ASK FOR ADVICE

Over the years, you may struggle with asking people for help and advice.

A difference in life experience, age, or culture, is no impediment to offering help. Nor should it prevent you from asking. On the contrary, working toward a common goal bridges so many irrelevant differences. The satisfaction in crossing that bridge reiterates how important it is to remember that more unites us than divides us.

Oftentimes, people are more willing to help than you realize. Further, people love to help those who help themselves. Whether that is with an opportunity, or simply by lending an ear whilst you enjoy a cup of coffee together. Sometimes, help means simply having someone to listen or bounce ideas off.

Help comes in varying forms, and sometimes you won't even realize it was help until much later down the road.

PART SEVEN

THE EASEL

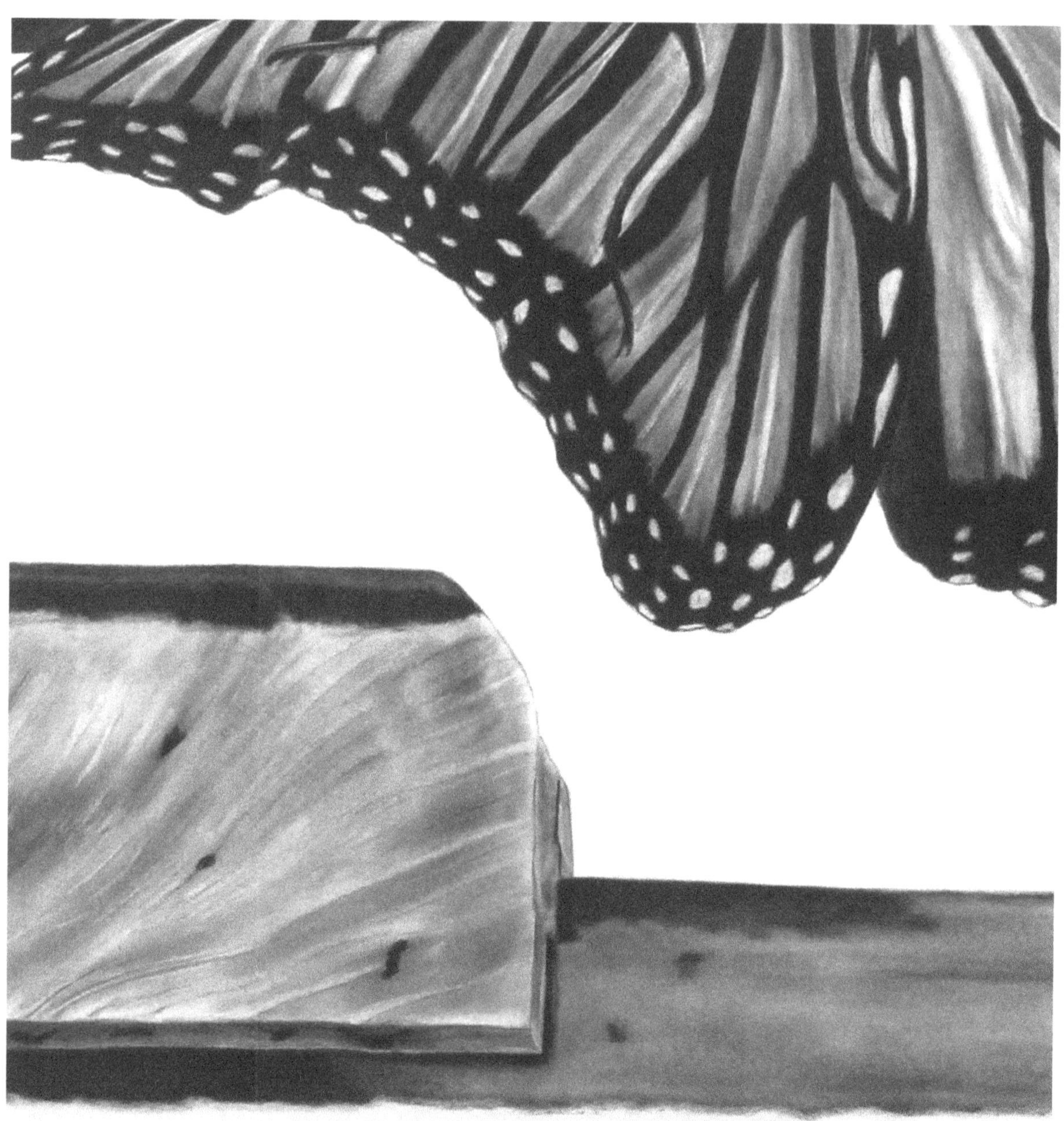

THE EASEL

A dear friend of mine has always told me, "Life is not a dress rehearsal."

She's spot on. It's the main event.

Seize the moment and embrace opportunities as they arise,

for you never know where that decision may take you.

You can always start anew by turning to a fresh page.

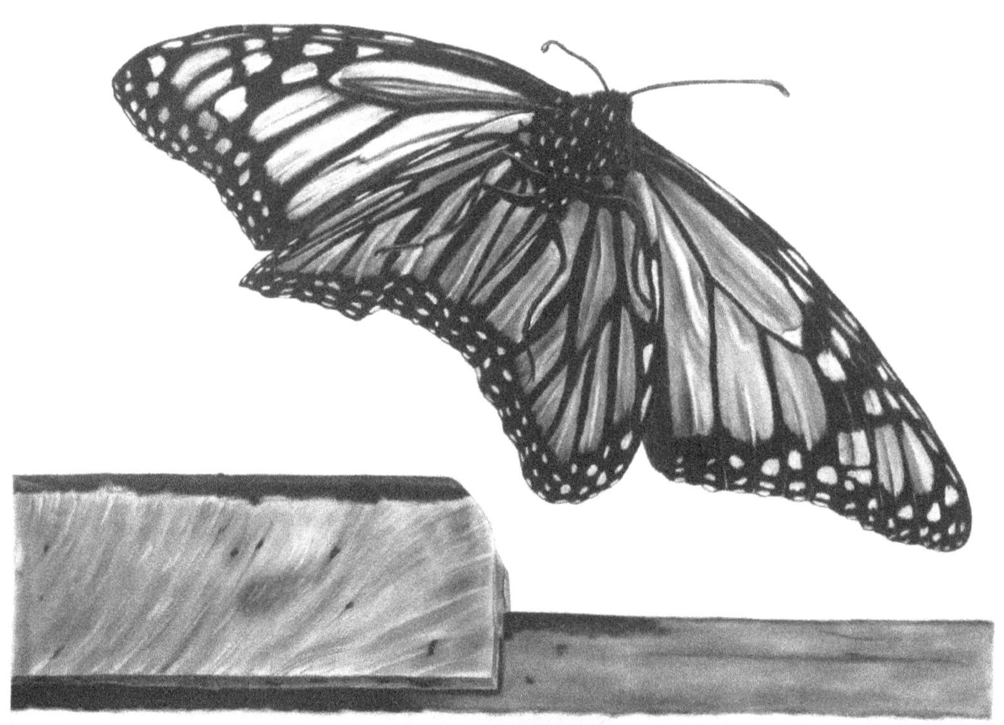

THE EASEL

YOU'RE QUITE RESOURCEFUL

An influential employer, a self-made billionaire, once complimented me, saying:

"You're quite resourceful, aren't you?"

This remark left a profound impact on me, as it was the most memorable compliment I've ever received in my professional career. The recognition I felt was palpable, signaling that someone had noticed the skills and traits I had honed over the years.

But how did this happen?

The comment left me to contemplate my career journey and the myriad of small lessons I'd learned along the way. I was struck by the number of valuable skills I had acquired, seemingly without realizing. Furthermore, I came to understand that many of the abilities I possessed were a direct result of past experiences, some of which may have seemed insignificant at the time.

This realization encouraged me to cultivate an appreciation for the diverse range of skills I had developed throughout my life. It also served as a reminder that, in moments of uncertainty or challenge, I could draw upon these resources to navigate complex situations with confidence.

The message I carry with me is simple: you are more resourceful than you think.

PART EIGHT

THE ROLL OF TAPE

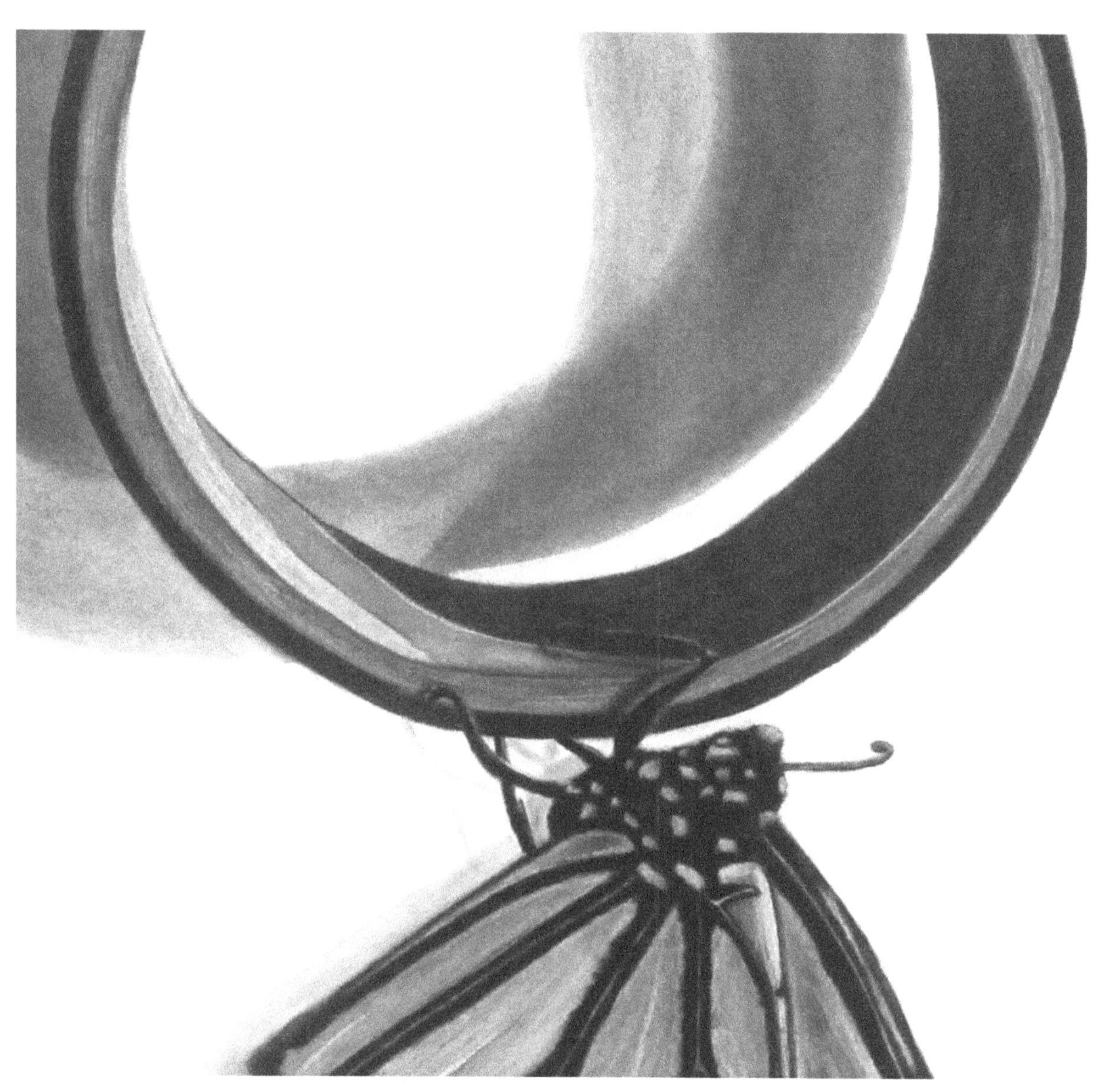

THE ROLL OF TAPE

You'll find yourself in seemingly sticky and challenging situations throughout life.

Knowing you can always count on yourself means you will never truly be alone.

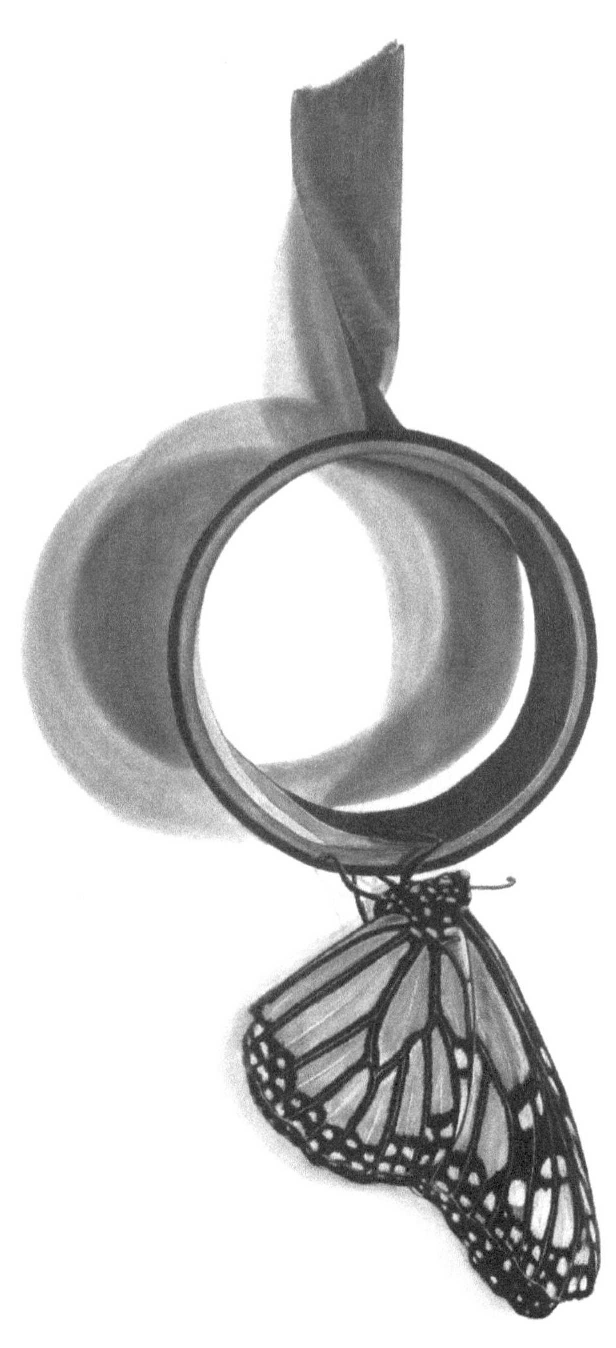

THE ROLL OF TAPE

PEOPLE WILL FORGET ABOUT YOU

Friendships and connections ebb and flow, existing for reasons, seasons, or lifetimes. Some friends may drift away or even turn against us. This can be a painful reality, but it's crucial to remember that these shifts are not personal attacks. Practicing self-preservation and remaining mindful of the transient nature of relationships will be helpful as we navigate life's changes and transformations.

Recognize that everybody is on their own unique path, each with their own story to tell: the star in their own movie. Furthermore, everyone is fighting a battle you have no idea about.

My guiding principle has always been to treat others as I would like to be treated: with kindness, respect, and empathy.

One of the most valuable lessons I've recently discovered is the importance of never dimming your light for anyone. For most of my life, I've consciously toned myself down, reluctant to share my stories or experiences for fear of making others uncomfortable. However, a mentor recently told me, "Katie, you may find inspiration in others, but please know that people are inspired by you too."

This revelation has empowered me to shine brighter and tell my stories with less fear of judgment or discomfort. I'm not suggesting we become obnoxious or self-absorbed. Rather, we embrace our unique experiences and constructively share them with the world. You never know who may need to hear your story, and in so doing, you may just inspire growth in yourself and others. So, shine bright and share those stories unapologetically.

PART NINE

THE CUPPA

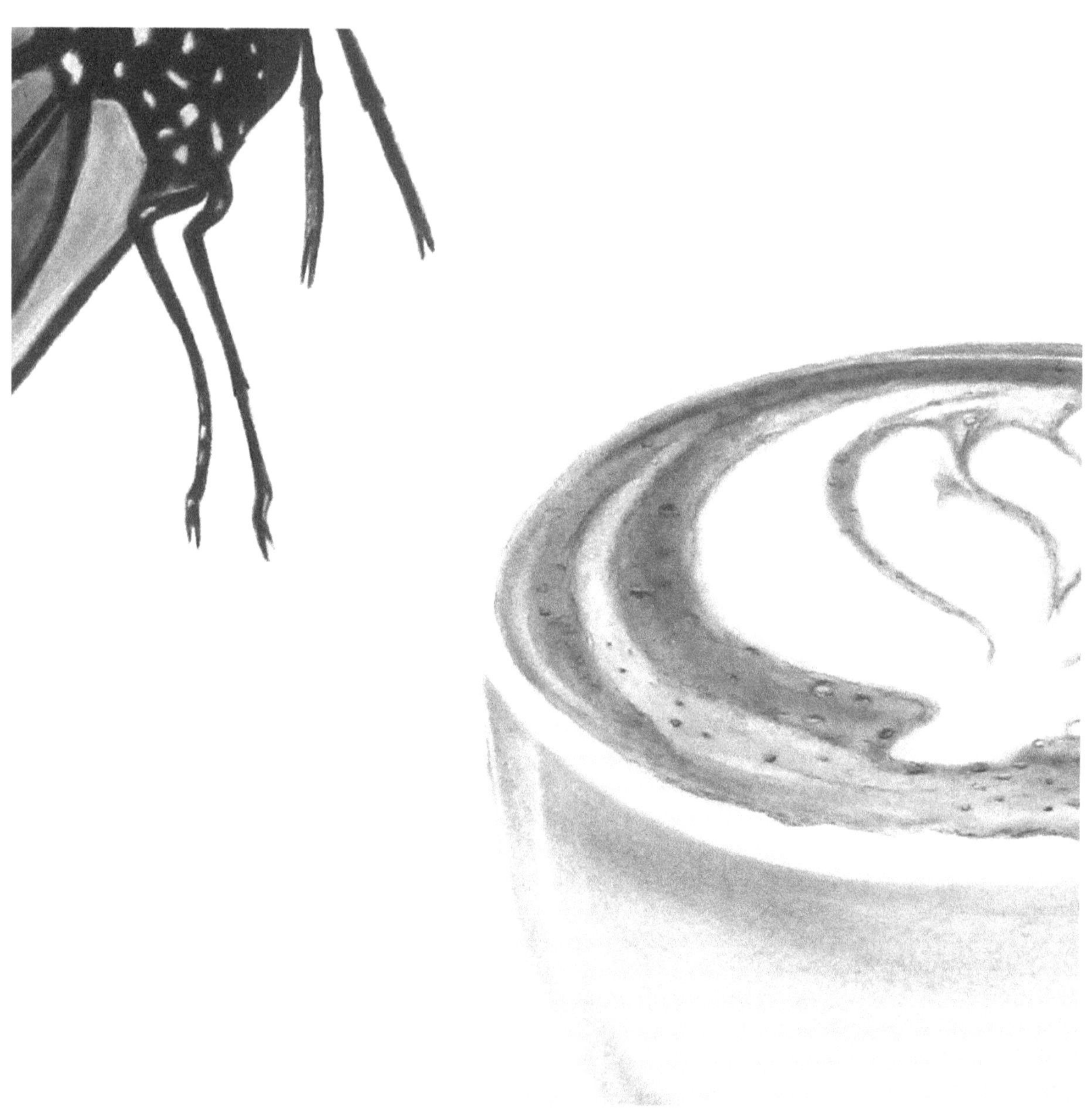

THE CUPPA

Savoring a cappuccino amidst birdsong and fresh morning air

is my favorite time of the day.

This moment, sharing a wholesome conversation with a loved one, or simply taking the

opportunity to be alone, reminds us of the importance of presence.

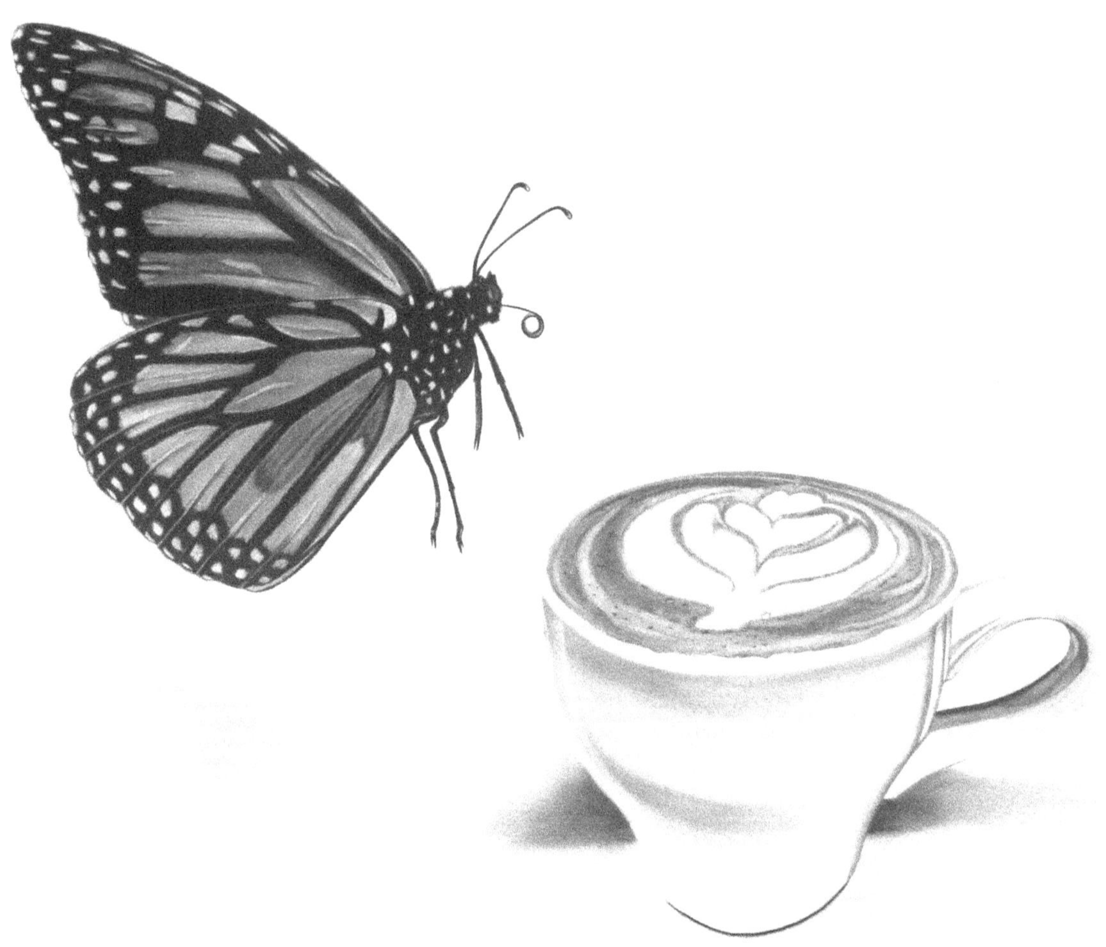

THE CUPPA

TRUSTING THE PROCESS

Disruptions to your presence will be constant and relentless. There will be moments where you want to simply give up. Take a break if necessary; regroup, but do not quit. Return to the cuppa. I need to remind myself of this more often than most would realize. I encourage you to persevere and embrace all that comes with the journey. Trust the process and resist the need to control everything.

Do not confuse the goal with the destination. The goal is tangible, and it is great to accomplish. However, the destination is fleeting; a mere stopover between journeys. The journey is where we live, day in and day out. Almost by definition then, that is what matters.

Make the choice to love yourself, to forgive yourself, and release desire. It is the joy that arises from embracing your authentic self that leads to ultimate freedom and fulfillment.

Remember that life is a road of growth, learning, and discovery. That road is already paved with happiness, if we decide to make it so. You'll find that happiness is not something that can be given to you by others, but rather something you create within yourself.

PART TEN

THE KNIFE

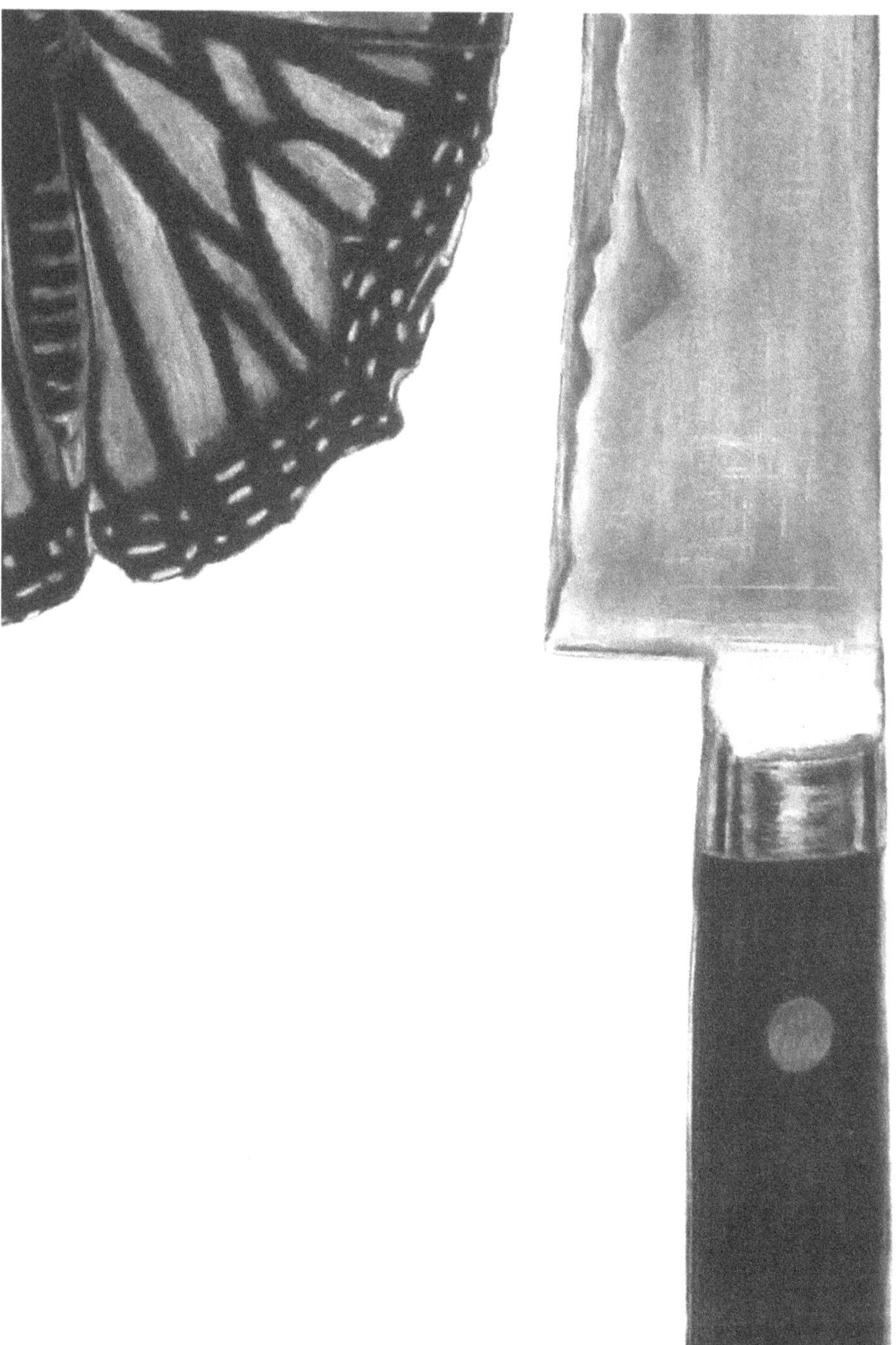

THE KNIFE

Cut out the negative self-talk. Cut out negativity in general.

Cultivate a positive mindset, knowing you are well-equipped to handle yourself.

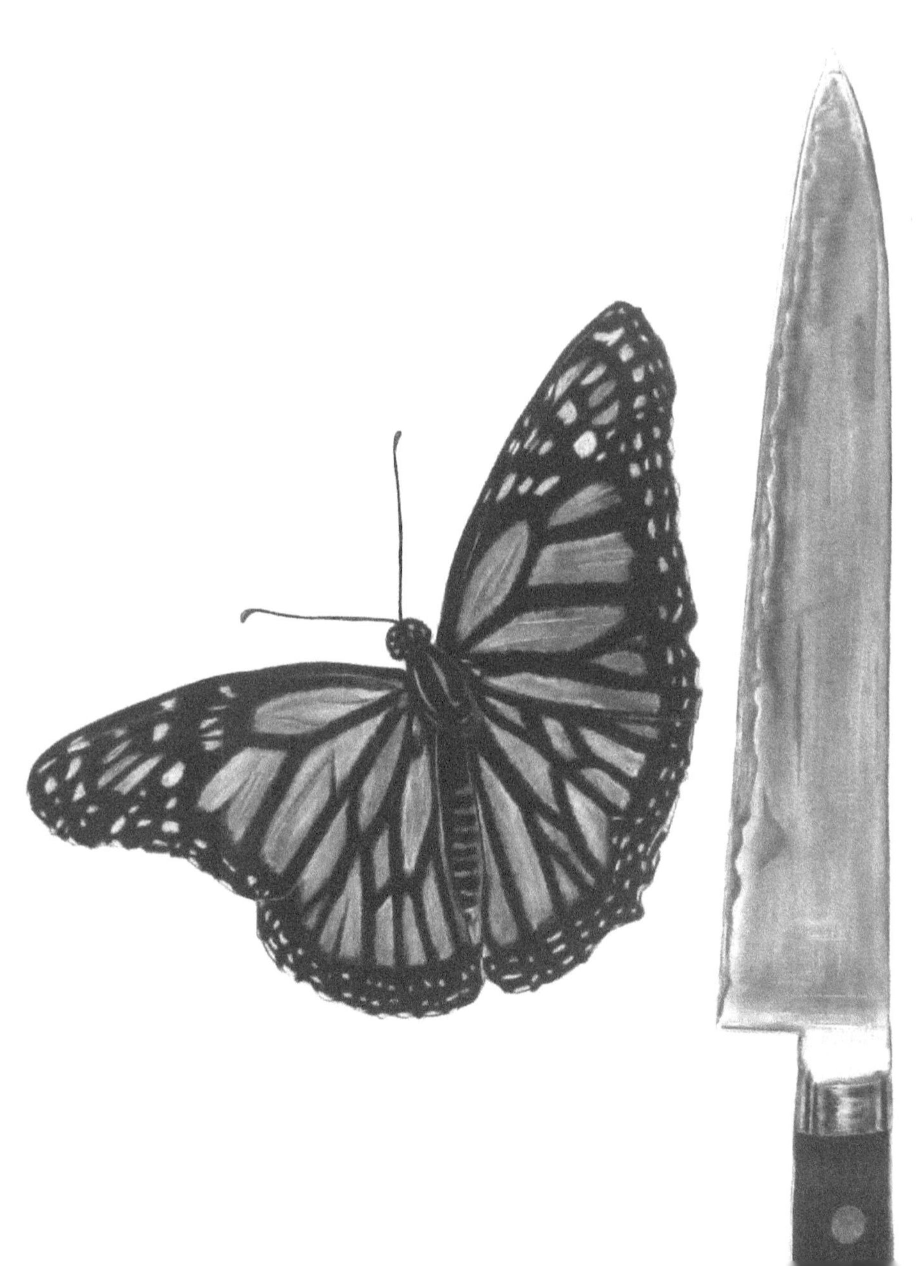

THE KNIFE

MAKING THE COMFORTABLE UNCOMFORTABLE

At some point, you may find yourself feeling stagnant and in dire need of change. The status quo no longer satisfies, and you might feel compelled to pursue a dream that's been on the back burner for too long. The prospect of change can be daunting, especially when others may view your current situation as perfect.

You'll know it's time for a change when the alternative consumes your thoughts and you can no longer ignore the calling. There will be an inexplicable voice within urging you to seek something new. This voice, I've come to realize, is the culmination of the lessons I've learned throughout my life. It is the deep trust in my intuition, and the crucial reminder that I am "quite resourceful, aren't I?"

Embracing the discomfort of change is essential, as it signifies the beginning of something new and exciting. It's a testament to your courage and willingness to take risks in pursuit of your dreams.

Remember: a comfort zone is a beautiful place, but nothing ever grows there. While it may not always feel pleasant, stepping out of the comfortable is a necessary part of our journey towards self-discovery and fulfillment.

PART ELEVEN

THE PASSPORT

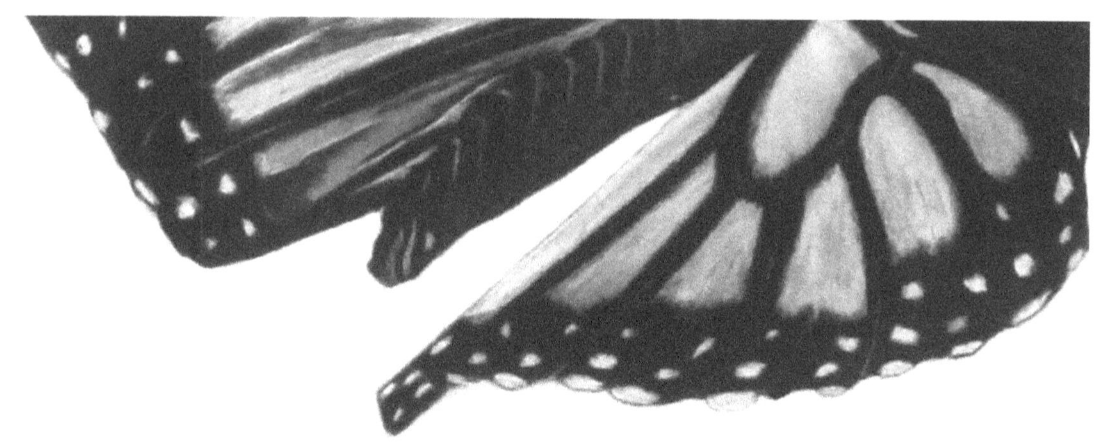

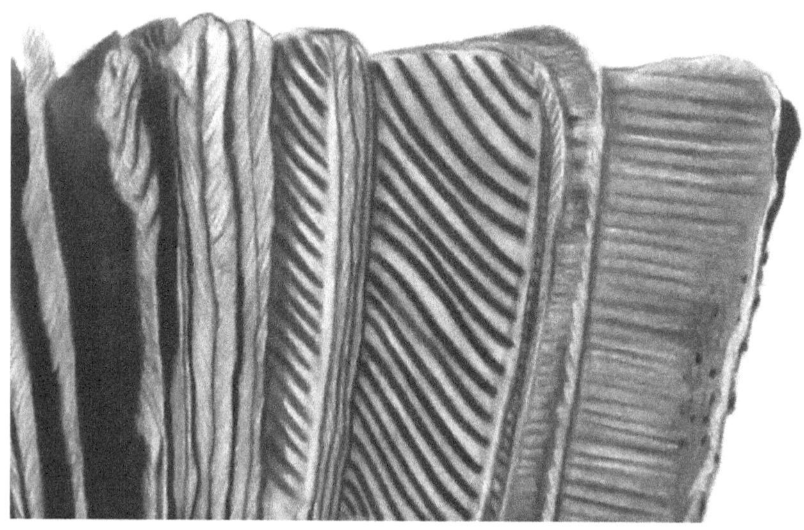

THE PASSPORT

If only that young girl knew what was ahead of her.

The dog ears of a life well lived. Smile at the imperfections.

A book that can tell a million stories.

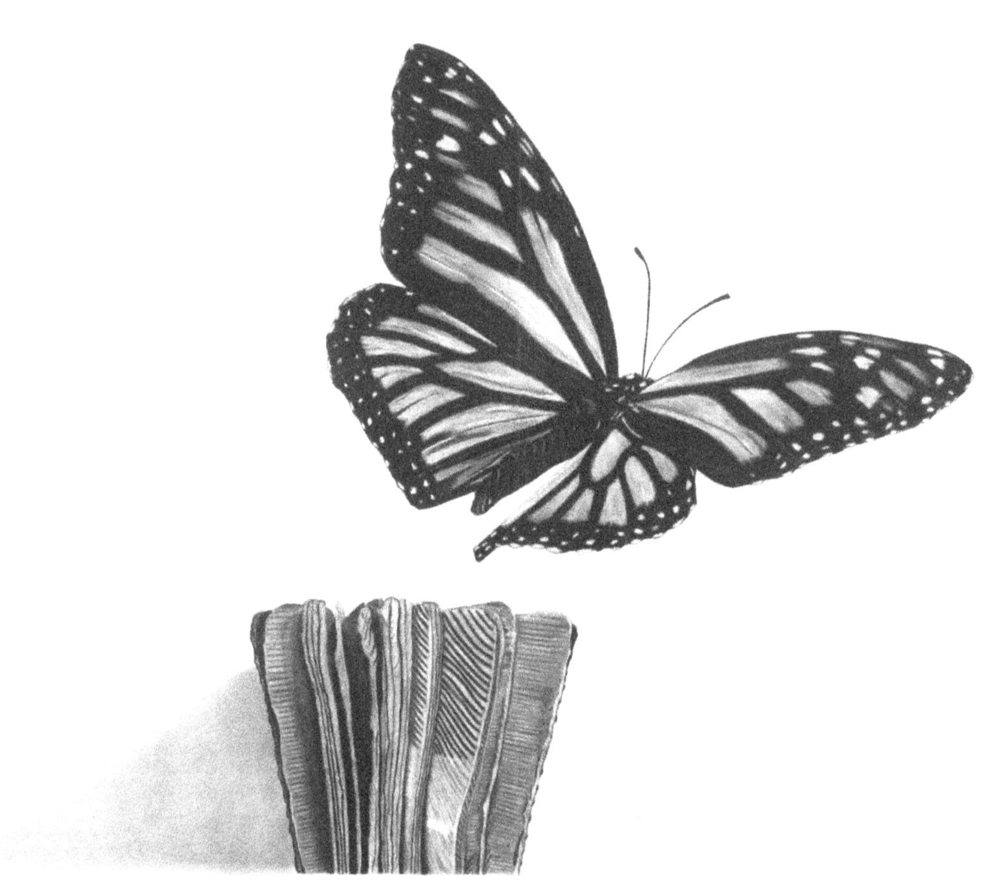

THE PASSPORT

JUST SAY YES

As I renewed my passport for the third time, I took a moment to reflect on the life I'd led up until that point. My first thought was, "My goodness, if only that girl knew what was ahead of her." There will be countless opportunities that present themselves throughout life, and I will reiterate the importance of embracing them. Say yes to opportunities, as you truly don't know where they will take you.

Throughout my years, I've found myself in the most extraordinary situations, and I've often had to pinch myself and ask, "How on earth did I get here?"

Upon reflection, I've realized that these seemingly serendipitous events were often the result of spontaneous decisions, chance encounters, and a willingness to take risks. I firmly believe that it's the courage to take chances and embrace uncertainty that has led me to where I am today.

Some may say that you're just lucky. Does luck not favor the bold?

Learn to think critically. Cultivate the ability to enjoy your own company. I consider myself fortunate to have developed the fortitude to trust my intuition and take the chances and risks I have. We create our own luck by seizing opportunities. There is beauty and power in having that knowledge. It is within us all to discover that realization and mold it to our will.

FINAL THOUGHTS

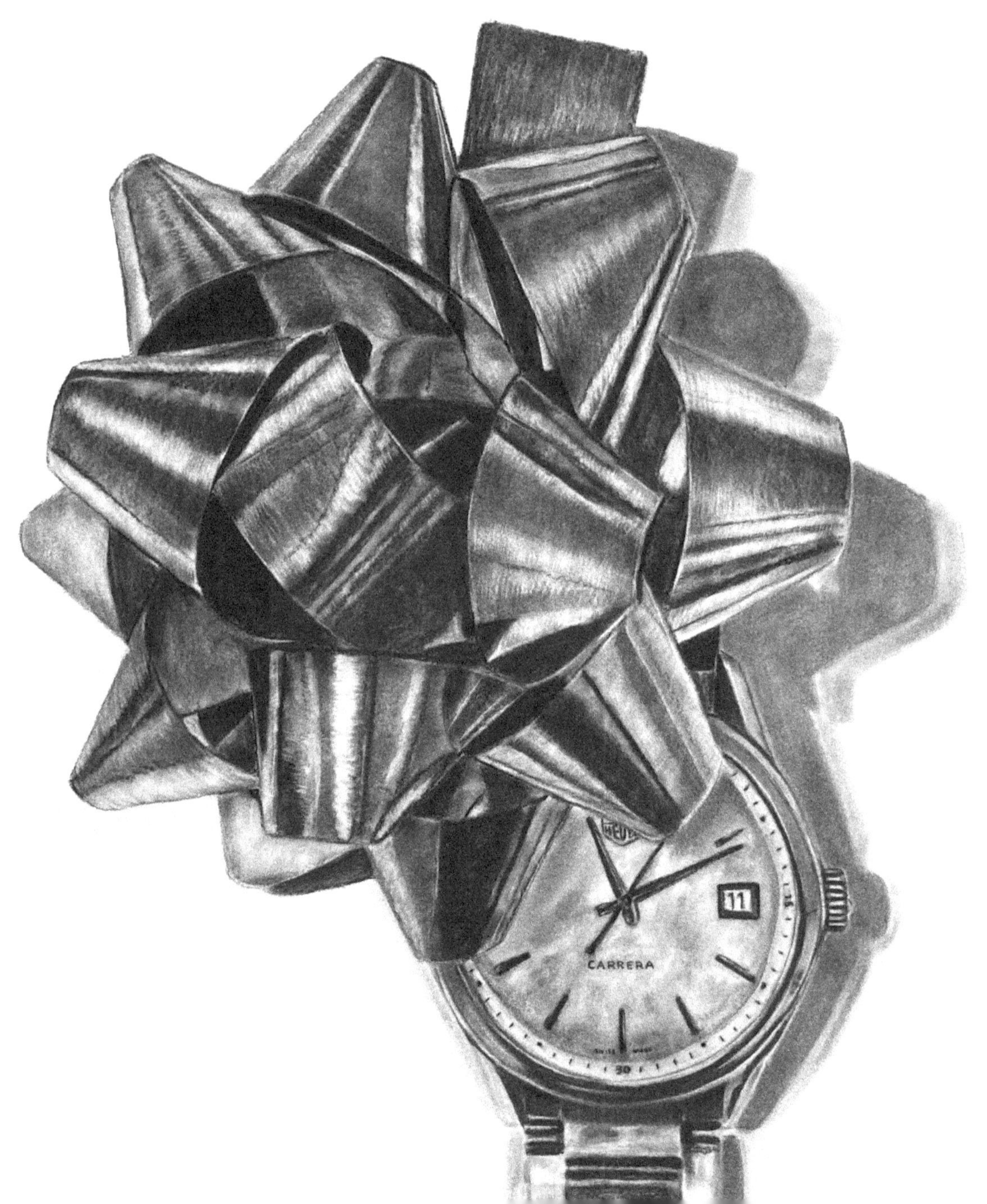

HEUER
CARRERA
11
SWISS MADE

TIME IS A GIFT

NOT TO BE SQUANDERED

In the transient nature of life, the future is uncertain.

What you have is this moment, and it's up to you to seize the

possibilities and shape your own destiny.

Embrace the enigmatic and take the leap into the unknown, for it is in this quest

that you'll discover the true rewards outweigh the risks.

With determination and a clear vision, you can achieve anything your heart desires.

The world is an infinite playground, ripe for the taking.

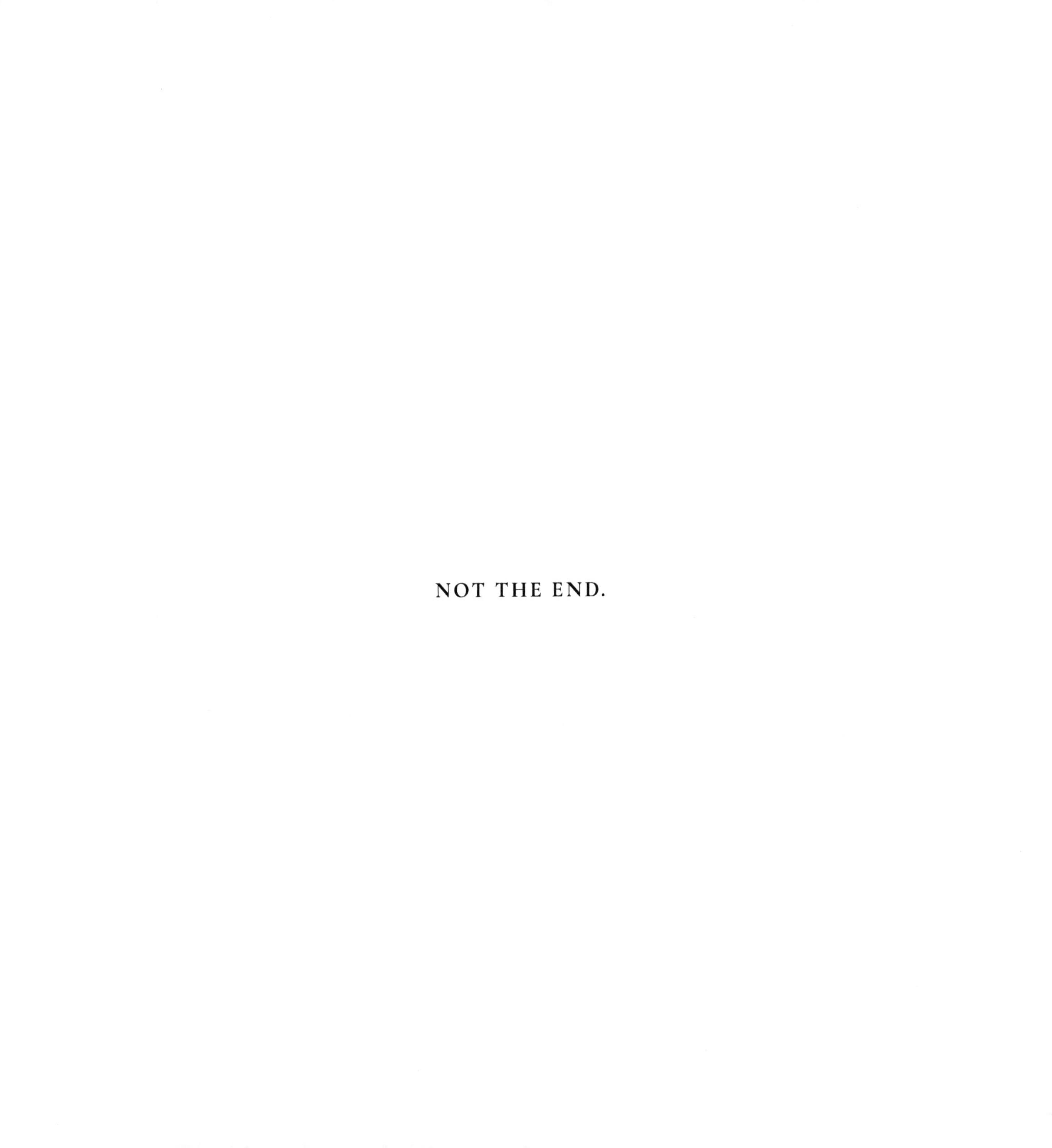

NOT THE END.

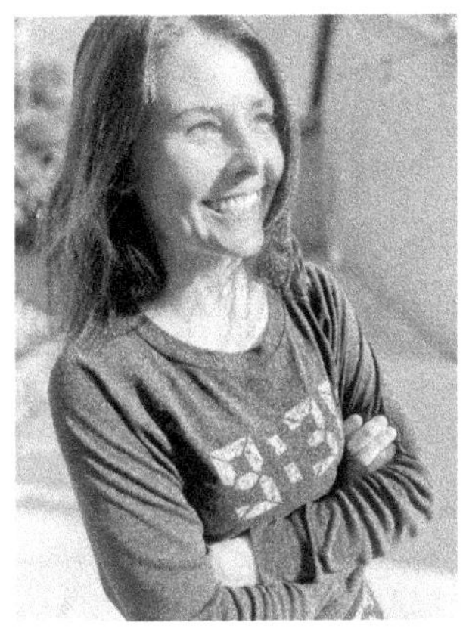

ABOUT KATIE

Hailing from the Whitsundays of Australia, Katie now calls Southern California home. Much of Katie's inspiration was born from her zest for life and thirst for adventure.

Growing up in a small town, Katie always had the desire to travel the world. With a focus on career opportunities that fostered this desire, she would explore many corners of the globe, by both land and sea.

This journey has been the crucible for her artistic expression: where obscure imagination meets real-life observation. It diverges from the conventional and sparks imagination, offering the viewer an alternative perspective to ponder.

With only a few rudimentary art classes under her belt, Katie's creative output is a testament to the power of self-taught ingenuity and perseverance. By sharing glimpses of her story and life lessons she's learned, Katie hopes to inspire others to unlock their own creative potential and forge unique paths.